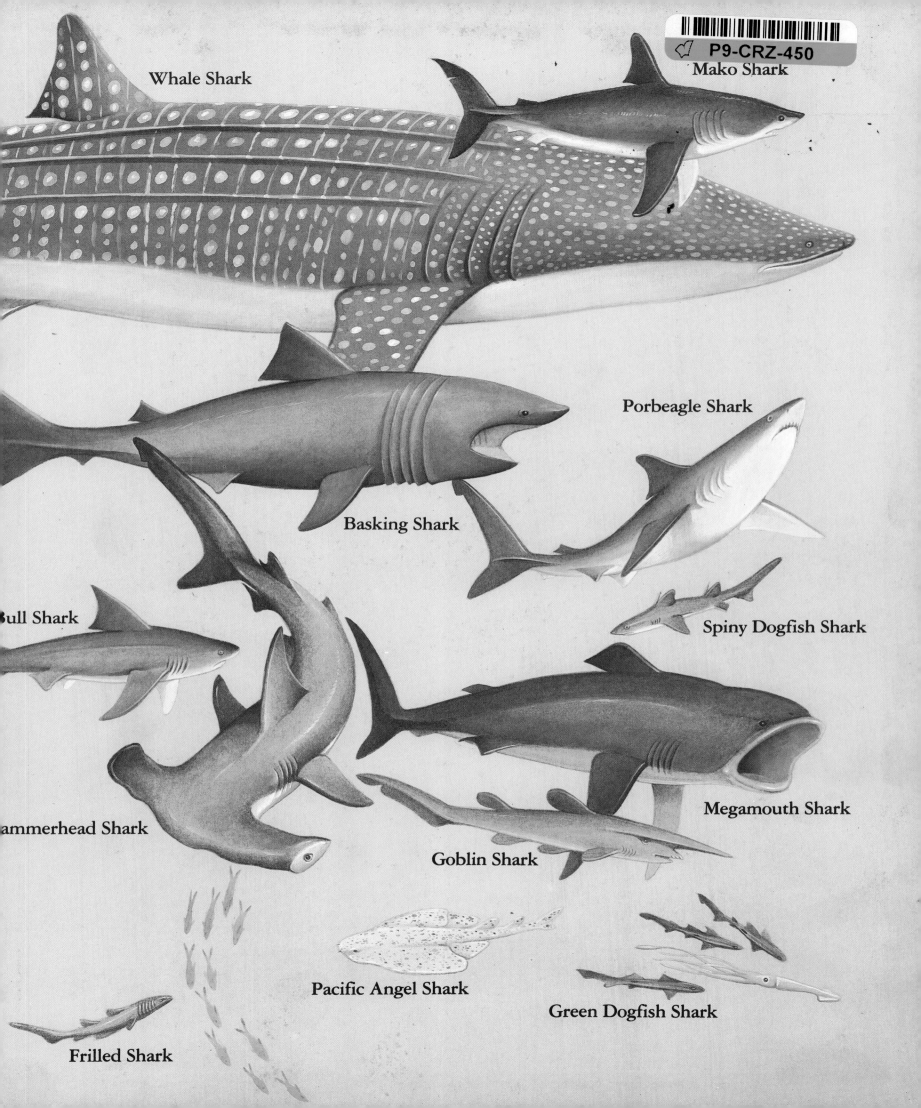

Whale Shark

Mako Shark

Porbeagle Shark

Basking Shark

Bull Shark

Spiny Dogfish Shark

Hammerhead Shark

Megamouth Shark

Goblin Shark

Pacific Angel Shark

Green Dogfish Shark

Frilled Shark

Sharks

Sharks

By Gilda Berger
Illustrated by
Christopher Santoro

Doubleday & Company, Inc.
Garden City, New York

Special thanks to Dr. Guido Dingerkus
of the ichthyology department, American
Museum of Natural History, New York,
for his careful review of the manuscript
and art for this book.

9 8 7 6 5 4 3 2

Library of Congress Cataloging-in-
Publication Data:

Berger, Gilda.
  Sharks.

  Includes index.
  Summary: Explores the world of
sharks, including historical data, current
information on shark research and
sightings, and descriptions of the behavior
and physical characteristics of twenty
major types.
  1. Sharks—Juvenile literature. [1. Sharks]
I. Santoro, Christopher, ill.   II. Title.
QL638.9.B47 1987   597'.31   85-29327
ISBN 0-385-23418-X
ISBN 0-385-23419-8 (lib. bdg.)

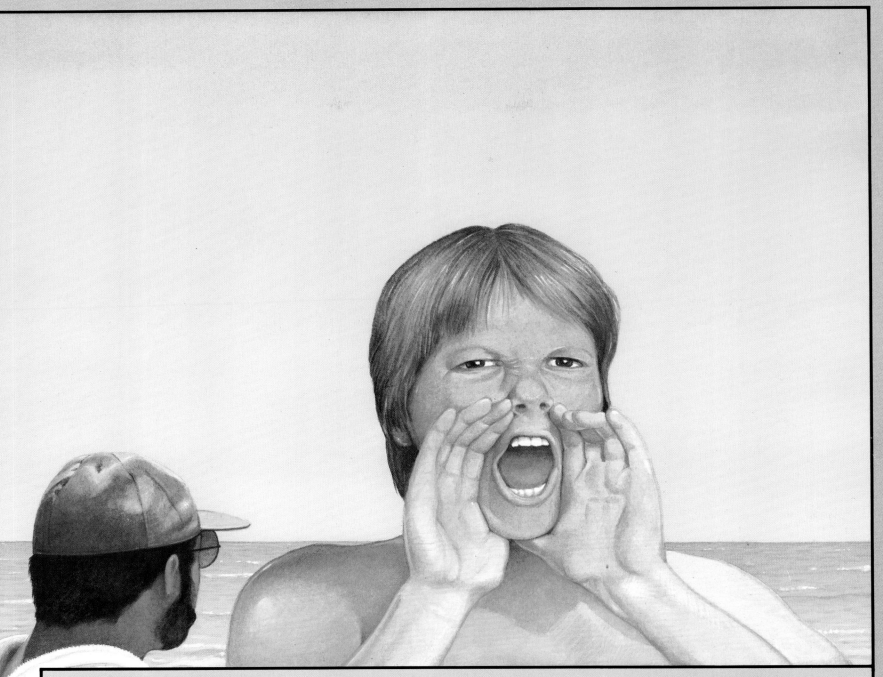

"*Shark alert! Shark alert! Everyone out of the water!*" the lifeguards shouted.

It was a hot Sunday morning, August 18, 1985. Hundreds of men, women, and children were swimming and playing in the waters off Coney Island beach in New York City. But at the warning everyone scrambled out of the sea. Nobody had to be asked twice. All were terrified at the thought of a shark in the water.

Within minutes a large, curious crowd formed along the shore. The lifeguards explained what had happened. A man in a fishing boat had caught a shark, but it had broken free and darted away. After the fisherman radioed his report to land, the guards cleared the water.

For three hours the bathers lingered on the hot sand. They watched the police helicopter and Coast Guard boats hunt for the shark.

By early afternoon the police and Coast Guard gave up the search. The shark was nowhere to be seen. The lifeguards sounded the all-clear. "The alert is over," they said. "The shark is gone."

Some people drifted back into the water. But many still wondered: What kind of animal is a shark? How and where do sharks live? Are all sharks killers? Is there any protection against shark attack?

Those Amazing Sharks

Everyone knows that sharks can be dangerous. But not everyone knows how fascinating they really are.

Did you know, for example, that sharks come in all sizes? One of the smallest, the dwarf shark, is only about six inches long. You could easily hold it in the palm of your hand. The largest, the whale shark, may reach a size of sixty feet. It is bigger and heavier than a trailer truck! But a typical shark, such as the sand shark, is perhaps six to seven feet long and weighs about 250 pounds.

There are sharks in every ocean—from warm tropical seas to cold arctic waters. One species even spends much of its time in rivers and freshwater lakes. A few swim in water so shallow that their backs and fins stick up out of the water. Others are found only in the deepest parts of the ocean, down to two miles below the surface. Certain types travel alone, while some move in groups, or *schools.*

Dwarf Shark

Mako Shark

Sharks are among the oldest beings that still exist on earth. They first appeared about 350 million years ago. Sharks are far older than humans who have been around for less than 5 million years. They even predate dinosaurs, which came into existence 225 million years ago.

Why have sharks lasted so long? Probably because they are so well suited to live under the water.

Sharks are built to feed on every living creature in the sea, from the weakest to the most powerful. Their mouths are lined with thousands of very sharp teeth. You could get a bad cut just by running a finger lightly along an edge. Sailors sometimes use shark teeth for shaving.

Worn teeth are constantly falling out. But all sharks have many extras. The teeth are arranged in four to twelve rows. They move forward like the steps in an escalator. As soon as one tooth falls out, another moves up to take its place. In ten years a shark can go through twenty thousand teeth!

Divers find large numbers of shark teeth of all sizes and shapes on the ocean floor. Some are long and pyramid-shaped, with jagged, sawlike edges. They are used for cutting and ripping. Others are slender and fanglike, and they are good for grasping. There are also blunt, flat teeth for crushing the shells of crabs, lobsters, clams, and other shellfish.

You may think it odd that the shark's mouth is on the underside of its head. Doesn't this make biting difficult? No, it does not. The jaw is hinged to let the

Magnified view
of shark denticles

shark open its mouth very wide. As it opens, the jaws push forward. That brings the mouth to the front of the head.

When the shark shuts its jaws, the teeth come together very hard, slicing through flesh or bones like a hot knife through butter.

But teeth and jaws are not the shark's only weapons. A rough outer layer of sharp spikes called *denticles* covers its body like a coat of nails. Any creature who rubs against the shark's skin the wrong way is soon badly scraped and bleeding.

Sharks are also very well equipped for swimming. Most have long, sleek, cigar-shaped bodies that enable them to glide easily through the water. The powerful tail sweeps back and forth to propel them forward. They use the two large *pectoral,* or chest, fins that extend out from the chest for steering. The rear fins balance their bodies like wings do on airplanes.

Most sharks cruise along at a speed of about two or three miles an hour. But when they are closing in on their prey they can reach

speeds of over forty miles an hour.

Unlike most other fish that have skeletons made up of bones, a shark has no bones in its body. Its skeleton is made of cartilage, similar to the bendable material that supports your nose and ears. A cartilage skeleton makes the shark able to twist and turn its body easily in the water.

Sharks also differ from other fish in the way they give birth to their young. Most female fish produce millions of eggs. The eggs are fertilized in the water by the males and only a few ever hatch. Some female sharks lay eggs. But most produce eggs that are fertilized and grow into young sharks inside the mother.

Almost all of the shark young, called pups, survive. Since the pups are born quite large and are equipped with razor-sharp teeth, they are able to care for themselves right from the start. Sharks usually live at least twenty to thirty years.

Most sharks swim with their mouths open all the time. As they move forward, water flows in. The water passes over their gills, bringing them oxygen. These sharks must keep swimming or they stop breathing. They swim day and night, from birth until death—even when they are asleep!

Sharks also have to keep swimming to stay afloat. If they don't, they sink to the ocean bottom.

Not long ago, a shark was caught and brought to an aquarium. It was almost dead when it arrived. To bring it back to life, aquarium workers pulled the shark through the water, forcing water over the gills. Soon the shark began to swim by itself.

Sharks do not usually survive very long in captivity. Some have been

taught to follow a maze, but rarely can a shark be tamed. No matter how long they are kept captive, they remain wild beasts of prey.

Sharks are nearly always hungry. They search for food all the time. Big and little fish, shellfish, and tiny ocean plants and animals, called *plankton,* make up their diet. Like some other animals that eat their own kind, certain big sharks also eat smaller sharks. It's interesting, however, that the giant of the shark world —the whale shark—eats the smallest prey—plankton.

Actually, sharks will eat just about anything they can find in the water—from garbage to humans. Among the unbelievable junk that has been removed from some sharks are license plates, beer bottles, and a chicken coop, with feathers and bones still inside! The stomach of a large tiger shark caught off Australia, for example, contained an entire goat, a turtle, a cat, three birds, many fish, and a six-foot shark. Another tiger shark in the Philippines had nine shoes, a belt, and a pair of men's trousers in its stomach.

Some experts call sharks "swimming noses." Two thirds of the shark brain is devoted to the sense of smell. This amazing ability helps sharks find their prey. The nostrils are located on the underside of the snout. With them a shark can detect a few drops of blood in the water from a mile away!

Once it picks up the scent, the shark swims toward the source. As it gets close, the shark depends more on its eyes. In the past scientists thought that sharks did not have very good vision. Now they believe sharks can see quite well. The eyes can locate objects up to fifty feet away. Some sharks can also adjust their eyes quickly.

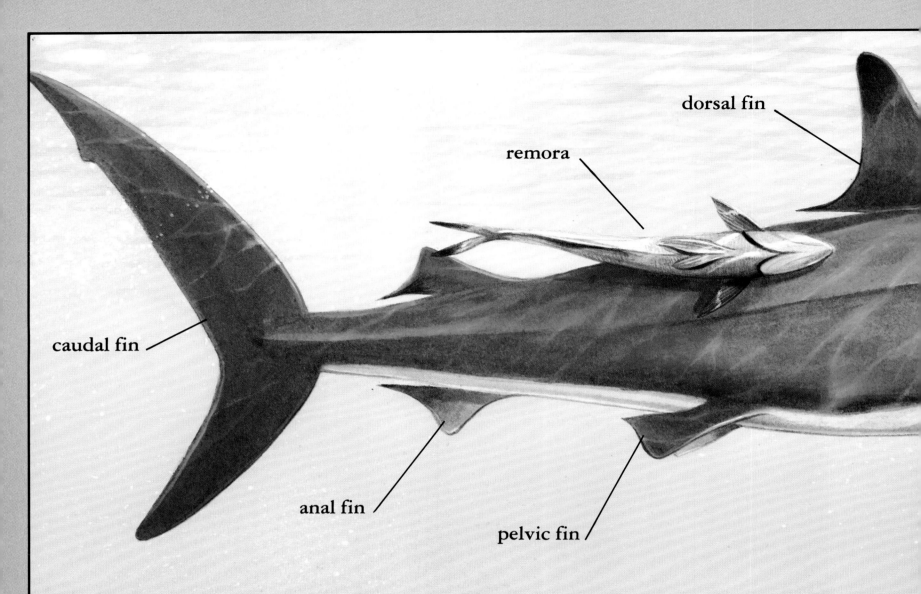

dorsal fin

remora

caudal fin

anal fin

pelvic fin

They can see at the surface of the water where it is light, as well as in the depths where it is always dark.

Sharks do not have outside ears like us. But they hear extremely well. Their "ears" are actually a tube running under the skin of their heads and bodies. The sound waves travel into the shark's skull along this tube. Scientists have tested sharks' hearing by making different kinds of sounds underwater and have discovered that sharks can pick up even the softest and most distant sounds.

The *lateral line* is an extension of the shark's "ears." It lets sharks feel vibrations or pressure changes in the water. The tubelike lateral line runs along the shark's sides, just beneath the skin. Any disturbance in the water changes the pressure on the liquid in this organ. The shark senses these changes and swings into action.

Sharks can quickly pick up the movement of a wounded fish, for example. Suppose someone hooks a fish. The fish flings itself about in the water to get off the hook. A shark can sense the fish's vibrations at great distances.

It heads straight for the struggling fish, and often before the catch can be pulled out of the water, the shark has bitten off a mouthful.

The *ampullae of Lorenzini* is another very useful organ. It is made up of little sacks filled with a jellylike material. This organ allows the shark to detect the tiny amount of electricity given off by all living beings. The ampullae are located in the shark's head, with very narrow openings to the outside.

The ampullae are particularly helpful in

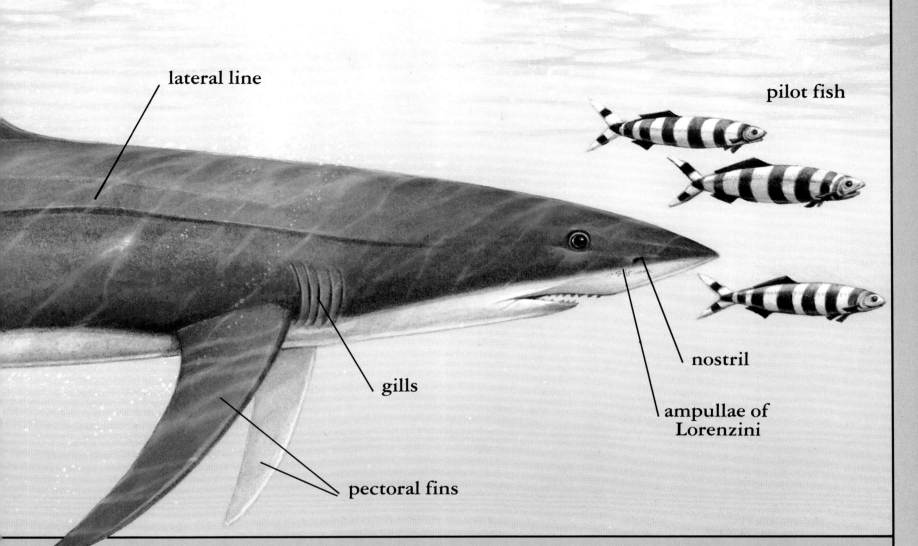

lateral line

pilot fish

gills

nostril

ampullae of
Lorenzini

pectoral fins

finding lobsters, crabs, and
other animals that live on
the bottom of the sea. These
slow-moving creatures often
hide in rocks and weeds.
They are hard to see or hear.
But like other animals, they
give off tiny amounts of
electricity. Thus sharks are
able to catch prey that most
other hunters in the sea
don't even know are there.

Having found its victim,
the shark stalks it through
the water. Practically
nothing can stop a shark
from satisfying its appetite.
Sharks have been struck
with harpoons, shot with
bullets, or pierced with

spears—but still they have
kept after their prey.

The shark often signals
the beginning of an attack.
First it lifts its snout and
arches its back. Then it
circles around, coming in
closer and closer. Next it
lunges forward, sinking its
teeth deep into the victim.

Madness and violence
break out if there is a large
victim, such as a porpoise or
whale, and other sharks are
nearby. The attack may
trigger a feeding frenzy. All
the sharks come together
and get very excited. They
thrash about furiously,
turning the water to white

foam. They bite and snap at
anything—the victim, the
other sharks, even them-
selves. In a few minutes the
frenzy is over. The survivors
glide away. Only the bloody
water tells of their wild
rampage.

Except for humans and
other sharks, the shark has
no real enemies. In fact, two
trusty mates accompany
many sharks wherever they
go. The *pilot fish* is a small,
dark fish that darts around
the slow-moving shark. It is
like a motorcycle escort for
a big limousine. Originally it
was thought that sharks had
poor vision and depended on

these fish to guide them. Now it seems that the pilot fish offers nothing to the shark—except a meal if the pilot fish is not careful.

The sharksucker or more correctly, the *remora,* is the shark's other companion. The remora does not swim alongside the shark like the pilot fish does. Rather, it hitches a ride on the shark's body. It attaches itself to the shark by means of a large suction plate on the top of its head. Wherever the shark goes, the remora goes.

The remora's suction is extremely powerful. People have tried to pull a remora off a shark. But the suction plate rips off before the remora loses its grip on the shark. One kind of remora is called "the shark's wife." It eats the parasites and small shellfish that dig their way into the shark's skin and eyes. This helps keep the shark healthy.

Most people are afraid of sharks. They consider them the most terrifying of all living creatures. But few realize that sharks rarely attack humans. Human flesh is not a normal part of a shark's diet. Do you know that you are more likely to be struck by lightning *three* times than to be bitten *once* by a shark?

In fact, only thirty or so humans are attacked by sharks each year worldwide. Of these, no more than ten die of their wounds. Compare shark attacks with dog bites in the United States alone. About three million people are bitten by dogs every year, and approximately twelve of them die.

Nevertheless, attacks do sometimes happen. And

scientists study them to learn more about shark behavior. One well-known attack, with many witnesses, occurred on February 26, 1966.

It was two o'clock on a hot afternoon. Thirteen-year-old Raymond Short was swimming about thirty yards off the south coast of Australia in five-foot-deep water.

Suddenly Raymond felt a tug at his left thigh. Something seemed to be pressing against his body. He reached down to brush it away. To his shock and amazement he felt a big, deep wound in his leg.

Just as Raymond started to call for help he felt a pull on his lower right leg. He reached down again. This time he touched the hard, spiked skin of a shark. He tried to flee, but the shark's teeth remained stuck in his body.

While people on shore ran to his rescue, the terrified boy beat the shark on its snout. But the powerful creature did not loosen its grip. Raymond bent over and bit the shark's nose. Still it held on.

Mr. Raymond Joyce of the local surf club was the first to reach the boy. He tried to pull him to shore but could not. By then five other men were at the scene. They tugged and beat on the shark with their fists. They attempted to force open its jaws. One man even smashed the animal over the head with a surfboard. The creature didn't even blink.

Together the men dragged young Raymond—and the eight-and-one-half-foot great white shark—onto the beach. Somehow they pried apart the shark's jaws. Blood was pouring out of the wound on Raymond's left thigh. The flesh of his right calf had been ripped away. You could actually see his shinbone, with shark teeth marks along its length.

Raymond was rushed to a nearby hospital and the doctors began treating him at once. The young man survived. The shark died on the beach.

Since far back in history, people have tried to protect themselves against sharks. Japanese fishermen wore red sashes to keep sharks away. On the Fiji Islands, men kissed the bellies of captured sharks in the hope that this would stop shark attacks. Primitive Hawaiians used to worship the god of the sharks, Kama-Hoa-Lii. And people on the Solomon Islands flung pigs into the water as gifts for the sharks.

The modern search for ways to protect humans against sharks began during World War II. Many soldiers and sailors were badly injured or killed by sharks after plane crashes or ship disasters left them in ocean waters. In 1944 the U.S. Navy developed the Shark Chaser. The Shark Chaser looks like a bar of soap. The user swishes it around in the water until it dissolves.

The Shark Chaser is made up of two substances. One is a chemical that drives some sharks away. The other is a dark, black dye that makes it hard for the shark to see anything in the water. Unfortunately, the Shark Chaser does not work very well. Experience shows that the chemical and dye too quickly spread out and pass from sight.

Scientists today are trying to find something better.

Their latest discovery is a chemical found in deter-gents, known as SDS. They are now testing SDS to learn how well it works and how it should be used.

The expert diver and famous underwater explorer, Jacques Cousteau, has his own way of turning sharks away. He uses a "shark billy," a three-foot club tipped with a circle of nails. But Cousteau says that the sharks usually return.

Underwater shark cages are often used to protect scientists or photographers from sharks. Unlike zoo cages, the people are inside and the animals are outside. For the past twenty years, many observations and films of sharks have been made from these cages.

To protect bathers at beaches, engineers have set up barriers of rising bubbles or of electrical wires around the swimming area. But these devices don't always keep out the sharks. In fact, some species are actually attracted to the barriers. At some beaches, shark walls have been built. The battering of the sea usually breaks them apart in a few years. Most successful are large, heavy nets hung in the water. Sharks heading toward the swimmers get tangled in the nets.

Right now there are no really good ways to keep sharks away from where you are swimming or diving. Avoid swimming in waters known to contain sharks and *never* swim alone.

Remember that there are over three hundred known species of sharks, but only about twenty-five kinds attack humans. And most people escape unharmed from encounters with sharks.

Meet the Sharks

Some call the GREAT WHITE SHARK "the perfect killing machine." It is the most dangerous and awesome member of the shark family. The great white has many razor-sharp, jagged teeth, each between two and three inches long. They are set in a wide mouth which is always slightly open in a clownlike grin. You can tell the great white apart from other large sharks by its sharp, pointed snout and long pectoral fins.

The great white is built to move fast and to devour its prey whole. An average great white is perhaps fifteen feet long and weighs about fourteen hundred pounds. The largest one ever caught was a full twenty-five feet long. Great whites will eat anything that lives in the sea. Their ripping teeth and powerful bodies can also sink boats and cut under-water cables.

Any large sea dweller—from a seal to a porpoise—can become a meal for a great white. This species, though, rarely attacks humans. Jacques Cousteau was once approached by a great white. The huge fish took a long and careful look at him, then turned and fled.

Great whites are few and far between. When one is spotted, it is usually alone.

They are most often found in deep water in the colder parts of the ocean. But they will swim to tropical waters during bitter winters when the water gets extremely cold. Great whites have been located along the coasts of the United States, from Virginia to Maine, and from California to Washington. Most attacks on humans have been in the waters off northern California.

Great white pups are under three feet long at birth, and each one weighs about thirty pounds. The young pups are dark on top with white bellies. As they get older, they turn a dull, grayish white all over.

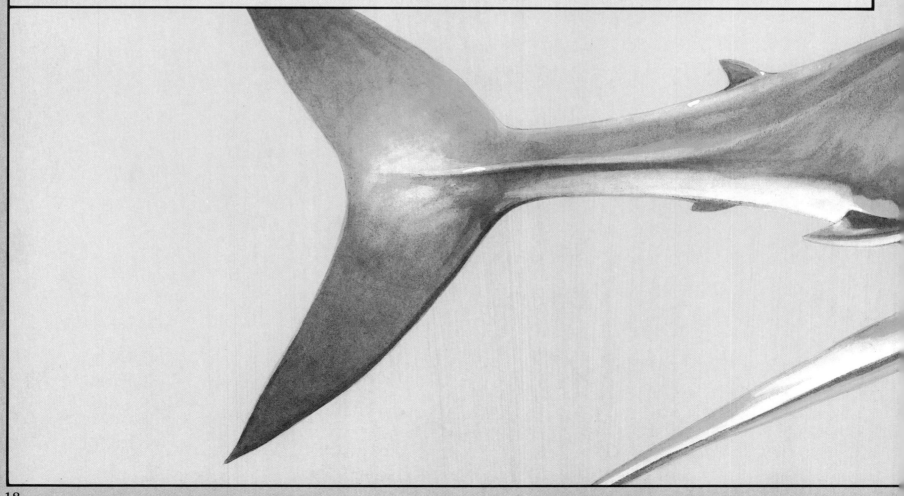

Great White Shark

Actual size of Great White Shark's tooth

The TIGER SHARK is considered by many to be the second most treacherous shark in the sea, next to the great white. However, it is probably even more of a threat to humans since it is often found in shallow water. Also, it will eat anything or anyone.

During the daylight hours tiger sharks are found far out from shore, away from swimmers and divers. But late in the afternoon they move toward the edge of the sea. And it is then that tiger sharks attack humans. Some victims have been bitten in water as shallow as three feet!

Tigers are not fussy eaters and are sometimes called "garbage can sharks." Their normal diet consists of fish, smaller sharks, crabs, turtles, dolphins, and squids. But they also like trash. The objects that have been recovered from the stomachs of tiger sharks make an incredible list. They include cans, shoes, hats, a bottle of wine, a coil of copper wire, and a tom-tom weighing eighteen pounds!

Round eyes, broad head, massive jaws, and a blunt snout make this shark easy to recognize. Its name comes from the tigerlike brown stripes on the backs of the young sharks. The stripes, however, fade with age.

Usually about twelve feet long from snout to tail, it can grow as long as eighteen feet and weigh nearly two thousand pounds. Tigers may have as many as eighty pups in a litter, but about a dozen is more usual. When they are born, each one is about the size of a house cat.

BULL SHARKS have very bad reputations. These fierce, aggressive fighters are thought to have injured and killed even more people than the great white or tiger sharks. Usually they are found in shallow ocean waters. But they are also able to live for periods of time in freshwater rivers and lakes.

Few other sharks can survive in fresh as well as in salt water. Lake Nicaragua in Central America, for example, is home to many bull sharks. They are also found in other rivers and lakes in South and Central America, New Guinea, Africa, and the Philippines. Among rivers, the Mississippi, several smaller rivers in Florida and Louisiana, the Congo and Zambezi rivers in Africa, and the Ganges in India are known to contain bull sharks.

These heavy, solid-looking sharks, with their short, rounded snouts and small, staring eyes resemble cattle. Hence their name. An average bull shark measures ten or so feet in length and weighs perhaps four hundred pounds. Usually they appear slow and sluggish. But they can put on amazing bursts of speed when closing in on a victim.

The fifteen-foot-long HAMMERHEAD SHARK gets the prize for being the strangest-looking of all sharks. Instead of a pointed or rounded snout, the hammerhead has a broad, three-foot-wide bar across the front of its head. Its eyes and nostrils are located at either end of the crossbar.

The T-shaped hammerhead uses its bizarre head to find food. As this shark swims, it swings its head from side to side. With two eyes and two nostrils facing in opposite directions, the hammerhead covers a very wide area at one time.

The ampullae of Lorenzini also help it locate stingrays, a favorite food, which often lie buried in the sandy ocean bottom.

Hammerheads live mostly in warm waters all over the world. But in summer they migrate to cooler waters. These sharks often hunt in packs and seem to move in toward the shore in the late afternoon and evening. And it is at dusk that most hammerhead attacks on humans occur.

One famous attack involved Kenney Ruszenas who was diving in forty feet of water near Palm Beach,

Florida, on August 22, 1964. Kenney noticed a hammer-head, about eleven feet long, approaching with its jaws opened wide.

Just as the shark was about to bite, Kenney thrust his spear gun against the shark's bottom jaw. The shark veered upward over Kenney's head, twirled around, and returned. Kenney jabbed again with his spear gun. This time, though, it just slid off the shark's tough skin. Then desperate, Kenney pushed the beast away with his bare hands. To his surprise—and relief—the hammerhead just swam away.

In the 1930s and 1940s

fishermen hunted hammerheads. Their livers were used as a source of vitamin A. A large hammerhead could fetch up to five hundred dollars. This ended, however, when scientists learned to make vitamin A in the laboratory.

One of the most beautiful of all sharks is the BLUE SHARK. It has a rich, dark blue back, brilliant light blue sides, and a snow-white belly. To add to its slim and graceful appearance it has a long, pointed snout. Average blues grow to be about ten feet long and weigh up to five hundred pounds. Blues are a very abundant species in both the Atlantic and Pacific oceans. A pregnant blue shark delivers as many as fifty pups at a time, each up to two feet long.

Since it is mainly a deep-water fish, there are few reports of blue shark attacks on swimmers. But experts think that blues have probably killed many victims of midocean ship or air disasters. The blue shark is a fast, powerful swimmer. It has been clocked at forty-three miles an hour. Its jaw is lined with seven rows of teeth, each as sharp as a knife blade. A single bite can rip out a huge chunk of flesh or an entire limb.

Blue sharks often follow oceangoing vessels. The crew can spot them because they swim near the surface. Their long, elegant fins can be seen sticking up out of the water. Blues are always ready to pounce on any garbage that is thrown over the sides. Some sailors believe that blue sharks will suddenly appear in the water when someone on board dies. The sharks are then said to swim alongside until the body is cast overboard for burial.

SAND TIGER SHARKS are terribly nasty and mean-looking. Their numerous teeth, although not very large, are sharp, thin, and fearsome to behold. Usually six to seven feet in length, the sand tiger shark has bright yellow, unblinking eyes and a powerful jaw.

Most fishermen hate this shark. It causes enormous damage when trapped. Not only does it eat the other fish in a net, but it rips the net apart. Sometimes it even sinks small fishing boats!

But aquarium visitors find the sand tiger shark exciting. It looks like their idea of a typical shark, with its rows of razor-sharp teeth, beady eyes, and prominent tail fin. Average sized, it also fits easily into most exhibits of living underwater animals.

A typical sand tiger shark litter is two pups. Shark history was made at Marineland in Florida on December 30, 1958, when the first sand tiger shark pup was born in captivity.

One look at the CARPET SHARK and you know how it got its name. A brightly colored pattern of spots and stripes covers its body, just like the design on a carpet. Fleshy tatters, called *barbels,* surround its snout, like a carpet's torn fringe. Unlike most sharks, the carpet doesn't have to swim to breathe. In fact, it lies like a blob on the ocean floor all day long. At night it walks around on its fins looking for small fish to eat.

The carpet shark hardly stands out from its surroundings. The colors and barbels blend in perfectly with the rocks, weeds, and coral of the shallow waters of the Pacific Ocean where it lives. And its slow motion makes it even harder to spot.

Because it is difficult to see, swimmers and divers often accidentally step on or kick a carpet shark. When this happens the usually quiet fish instantly flips over and buries several rows of needle-sharp teeth in the trespasser's leg. And it doesn't let go. Attacking carpet sharks have been shot, pounded on the head, or stabbed, but they have held on to their victims.

The largest carpet sharks are over ten feet. An average one is about half that length. In Australia the carpet shark is called the WOBBEGONG.

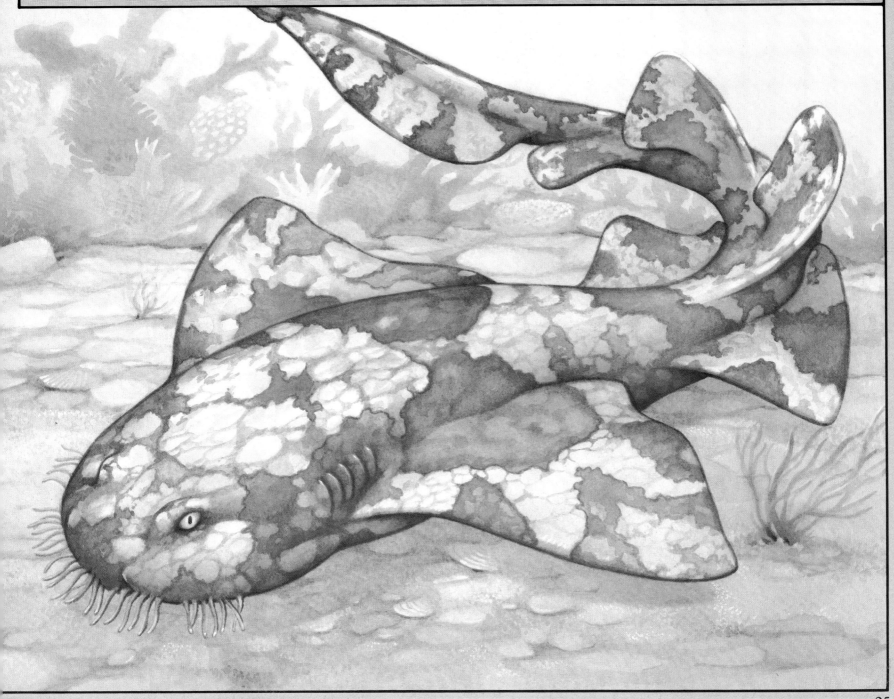

What comes to mind when you hear the name NURSE SHARK? Probably not a slow-moving, lazy fish that lives on the bottom of the sea. No one is sure why the nurse shark was given that name. Yet scientists do know a lot about the way it lives. It moves through the water like a snake and hides in reefs or underwater caves for long periods at a time. When it stirs, it searches for shrimps, lobsters, crabs, and sea urchins, which it crunches between its strong, blunt teeth.

A nurse shark lying quietly in the shallow waters looks quite harmless. But appearances can be deceiving. When one skin diver tried to "ride" a twelve-foot-long nurse shark, it whipped around and took a big bite out of his thigh. Many others, too, have learned not to disturb nurse sharks.

The OCEANIC WHITETIP SHARK is a dull olive color, except for the bright white tips on its fins. Up to thirteen feet long and thirteen hundred pounds in weight, these fish are very strong. They have been known to keep swimming or fighting even after being shot with several bullets. In battles with other sharks or large fish, oceanic whitetips always win.

There are more oceanic whitetips than any other large fish in deep ocean waters. They seldom come close to land. Perhaps that is why they have never been reported to attack swimmers or divers. But they are attracted to disasters at sea. Many victims of plane crashes or ship sinkings are killed by the jaws of these huge monsters of the deep.

The MAKO SHARK is a fierce fighter. When hooked, the slim, bright blue, silver-bellied mako struggles long and tirelessly. It can leap as high as twenty feet trying to break free. When chased by a motorboat, these fast swimmers have been clocked at over forty miles an hour.

Makos compete with fishermen for large catch like tuna, marlin, or swordfish. Often they help themselves to a fish on a line before the fisherman can pull it out of the water. People try to catch makos, though, because they are the tastiest sharks for eating.

Everything is graceful and beautiful about the mako—except its jaws. Eight rows of smooth, slender but very long sharp teeth that slant inward line its narrow mouth. The Polynesians of New Zealand valued mako teeth so highly that they made them into jewelry.

The PORBEAGLE SHARK is often mistaken for the mako, even though it is darker blue and less slender. Its teeth are also pointed and narrow but have small peaks, or *cusps*, on either side.

Among the fastest swimmers in the sea, porbeagles are found in all cold and temperate ocean waters. None has been accused of attacking swimmers. That is probably because the porbeagle hunts in deep waters, very far from crowded beaches. But it is not safe from human attack. People in England and Italy, for example, hunt and eat porbeagles.

The WHALE SHARK is the giant of the fish world. Bigger and heavier than some whales, it ranges between thirty-five and sixty feet in length and weighs from ten to fifteen tons. Its back, covered with yellow-and-white dots on a striped brownish background, looks like a giant checkerboard with a checker in each box. At the end of the enormous body is a long thin tail with a pointed fin—the clue that it is a shark and not a whale.

As you might expect, these giant sharks are very strong and powerful. A whale shark was once hooked through its back fin. But the shark took flight. For three hours it towed two steel-hulled boats, lashed together and carrying sixteen men, at six miles an hour!

Few people have had the awesome experience of looking into the mouth of a whale shark, which is lined with thousands of teeth. Someone who did compared it to looking into the front end of a jumbo jet engine. When the shark's huge mouth is open, and it usually is, a full-grown man could easily fit inside.

Despite its great size and power, the whale shark has an easygoing nature. Mostly it swims slowly and lazily just below the surface of the water. When approached, it

gives no sign of fighting or fleeing. It never attacks humans, or even large fish. Divers have often climbed on its back or hitched rides by hanging on to its back fin or tail.

Life demands little effort from the whale shark. The tropical waters it inhabits are teeming with food. Billions of tiny plants and animals flow steadily into its open mouth as it swims along. Inside its mouth the gills act like a strainer, or sieve. This sieve traps the tiny bits of food before the water passes out through its gill slits. An average-sized whale shark filters thousands of tons of sea water every hour.

Occasionally a whale shark stands on its tail and bobs up and down. As it does, it swallows whole schools of sardines or other small fish.

For a long time people did not know how whale sharks bear their young. Then in 1953, the captain of a shrimp trawler noticed an unusual-looking egg case in one of his nets. When he reached down he felt something kicking around inside. He opened it with a knife. An embryo, looking exactly like a miniature whale shark, flopped out. From that fisherman, scientists learned that baby whale sharks hatch from eggs laid in the water.

Like the whale shark, the BASKING SHARK is huge, slow-moving, and generally harmless. The largest ones are about forty-five feet long and seven tons in weight. They have five enormous gill slits that almost meet below the head. The gill slits make the shark look like its head is about to fall off.

Seamen long ago told of seeing giant sea monsters hundreds of feet long. Now we think that they were seeing four or five basking sharks swimming in a line, the snout of one touching the tail of the one in front.

About two hundred years ago, New Englanders hunted the basking shark. At that time, people still used oil for lamps and for making candles. They could get about six hundred gallons of oil from one basking shark's liver. Americans no longer hunt these sharks. But many who live in other parts of the world still catch them for their valuable oil.

Basking sharks like to swim together near the surface of the water. Sometimes a school of one hundred or more are found in the cooler waters where they live. They can draw four tons of water a minute past the thousand bristly gill rakers in their mouth. This traps large quantities of plants and animals inside. Keeping their huge bellies full is an activity that goes on without stop.

The THRESHER SHARK is about ten feet long. But its tail adds almost another ten feet to its overall length. Beware of this long and powerful tail. There is an account of a fisherman who leaned too far over the side of his boat. Before he knew what was happening, the tail of a thresher supposedly whipped out of the water and cut his head off.

Numerous experts question this story, however, because the thresher's tail may only be sharp enough to cause a bad bruise.

Actually, threshers do not usually harm humans. Mostly they eat small fish such as herring, bluefish, mackerel, and porgies. First they swim in circles around a school of fish, using their tails as whips to drive the smaller fish together. Once the fish are in a close group, the thresher charges in, its jaws wide open. It catches them easily, swallowing a few with each big gulp. The thresher then swings around for another tasty mouthful.

Threshers live a few miles offshore in all the temperate oceans and seas of the world. A litter usually contains two pups, each five feet long.

The MEGAMOUTH SHARK was not discovered until 1976 by sailors on a U.S. Navy research ship. The ship was cruising northeast of Hawaii when something was noticed tugging on the anchor line. When they hauled it in, they found a fourteen-foot-long, one-ton shark with a huge mouth and immense head. On the spot, the sailors dubbed it big mouth, or *megamouth.* And the name stuck.

For a few years, no other megamouths were seen. Then in November 1984, another giant specimen was caught near Santa Catalina Island off the coast of California. Scientists now hope for more sightings of this strange and unusual shark.

The SPINY DOGFISH SHARK must be handled very carefully because it has two poison spines on its back. It attacks by flinging itself with spines extended against its enemy. When a spine enters the flesh, a squirt of poison flows into the victim. No human has ever been killed by this poison, but many have been made very sick.

Spiny dogfish are disliked for another reason. Traveling in large packs, they consume many kinds of fish that people like to eat. If they are caught in a fishing net full of cod or herring, for example, they will gulp down many of the fish and destroy the net as well.

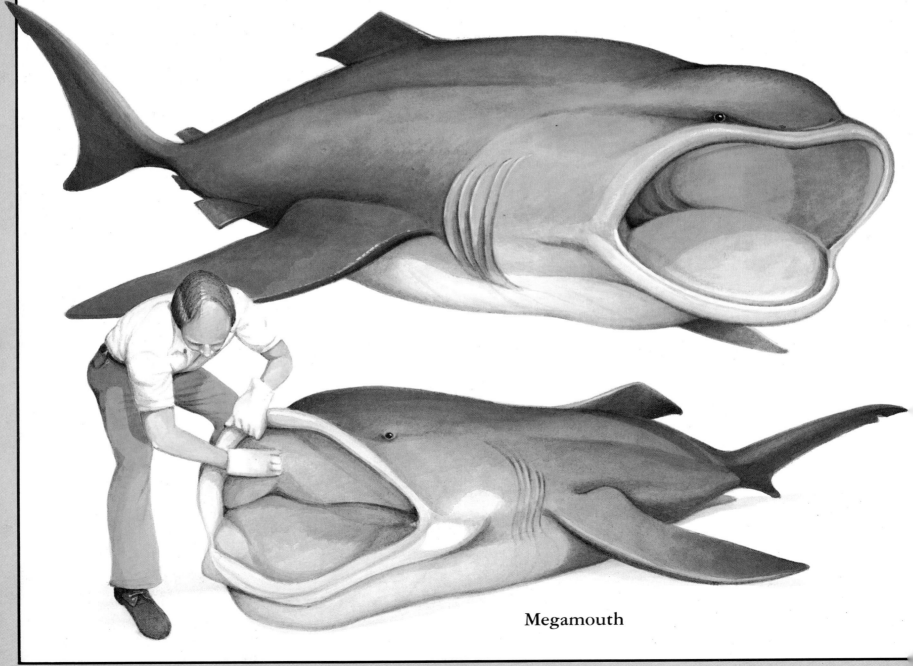

Megamouth

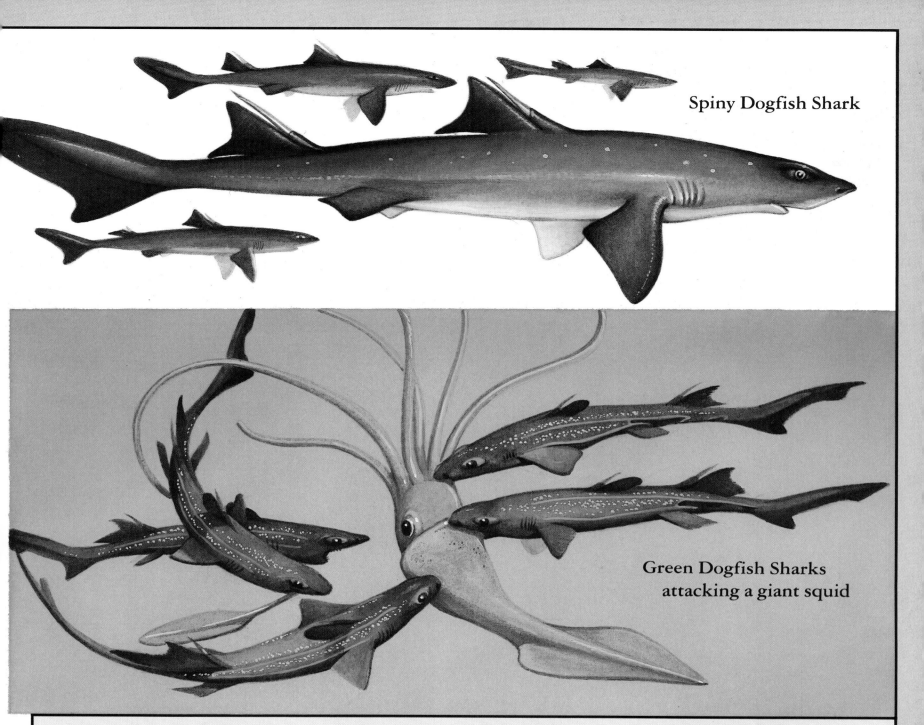

Spiny Dogfish Shark

Green Dogfish Sharks
attacking a giant squid

Europeans like to eat the spiny dogfish. The English sometimes use them in the dish, fish and chips. They also sell them in shops and restaurants under the names flake, rock salmon, or sea eel.

The spiny dogfish shark is about three feet long, weighs ten pounds, and is usually dull gray or brown in color. It holds the record for the longest pregnancy, or *gestation*, of any vertebrate— twenty-four months. That is even longer than the whale or elephant. When the female gives birth, she usually bears about five pups, each nine inches long.

The sight of a GREEN DOGFISH SHARK at night would surely startle you. A design of bright green glowing lights decorates its body. Scientists know that the green lights come from tiny organs called *photophores.* But they are not sure of their purpose. Some think that the glow helps green dogfish sharks keep in touch with one another in the dark reaches of the ocean.

Green dogfish are found in great numbers along the north coast of the Gulf of Mexico. There they feed on squid and octopus. Great numbers of green dogfish swarm over their victims and bite off chunks of their flesh with razor-sharp teeth.

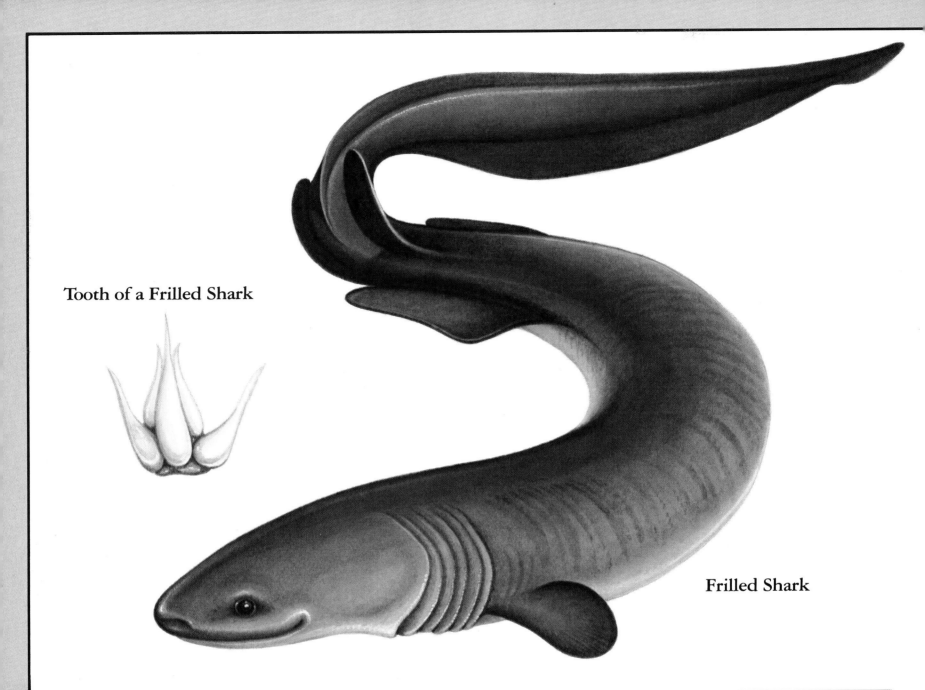

Tooth of a Frilled Shark

Frilled Shark

The gills of the FRILLED SHARK look like a collar around its neck. This shark has six large, raised gill slits instead of the usual five. The first gill actually circles its body. The other five are only on the sides.

The frilled shark hardly looks like a shark. Its oversized mouth is at the tip of its snout, not under the head. And its long narrow body and smallish head make it look like an eel or snake. But it surely has a shark's cutting teeth. Each one is tipped with three wicked-looking, needle-sharp points.

The frilled shark is brownish gray in color. It grows to a length of five or six feet and is about four inches around. Squid and octopus are its favorite foods.

The wide, flat side fins on the ANGEL SHARK remind some people of angel wings. Others think the fins resemble a monk's robes, so the shark is also called a MONK SHARK. But these sharks do not really look like angels or monks. They look most like the kind of fish known as skates or rays. An average angel shark is about four feet long and almost as wide across its fins.

This strange-looking creature is a slow, sluggish swimmer. It likes to burrow in the sandy ocean bottoms. But, like other sharks, it will snap and fight fiercely when annoyed.

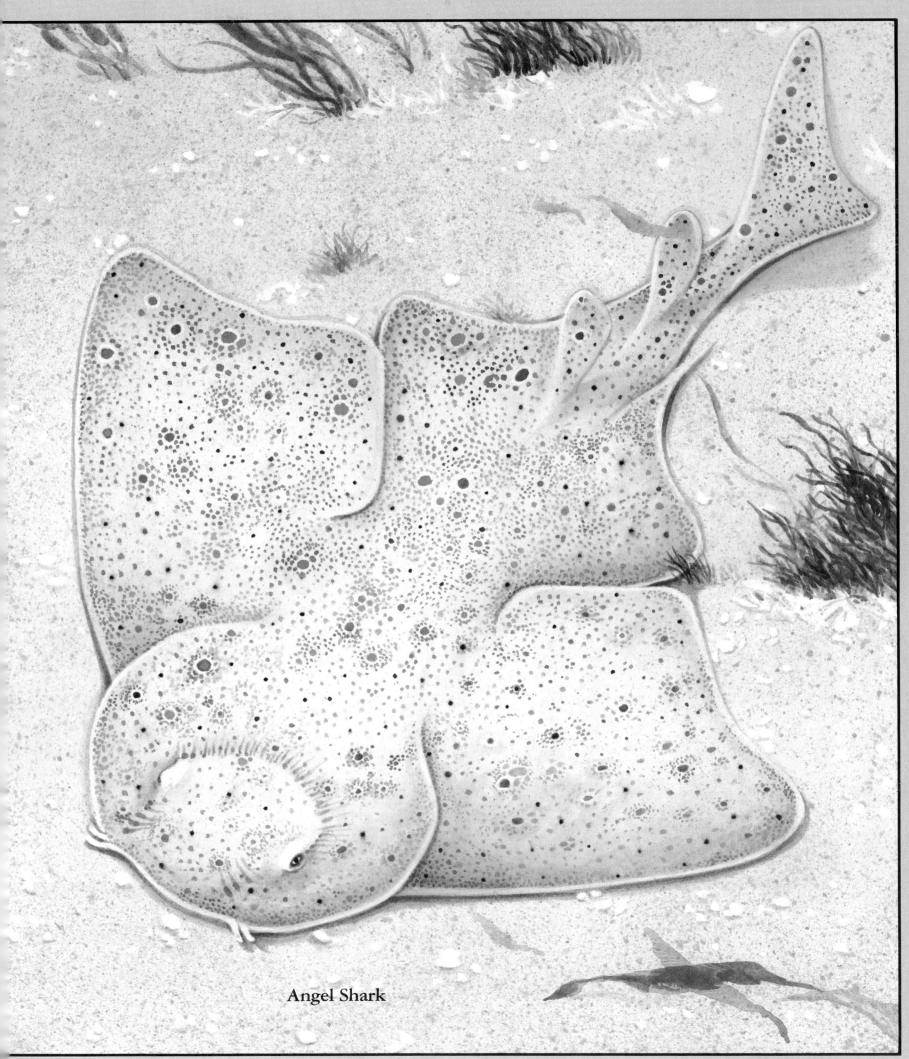

Angel Shark

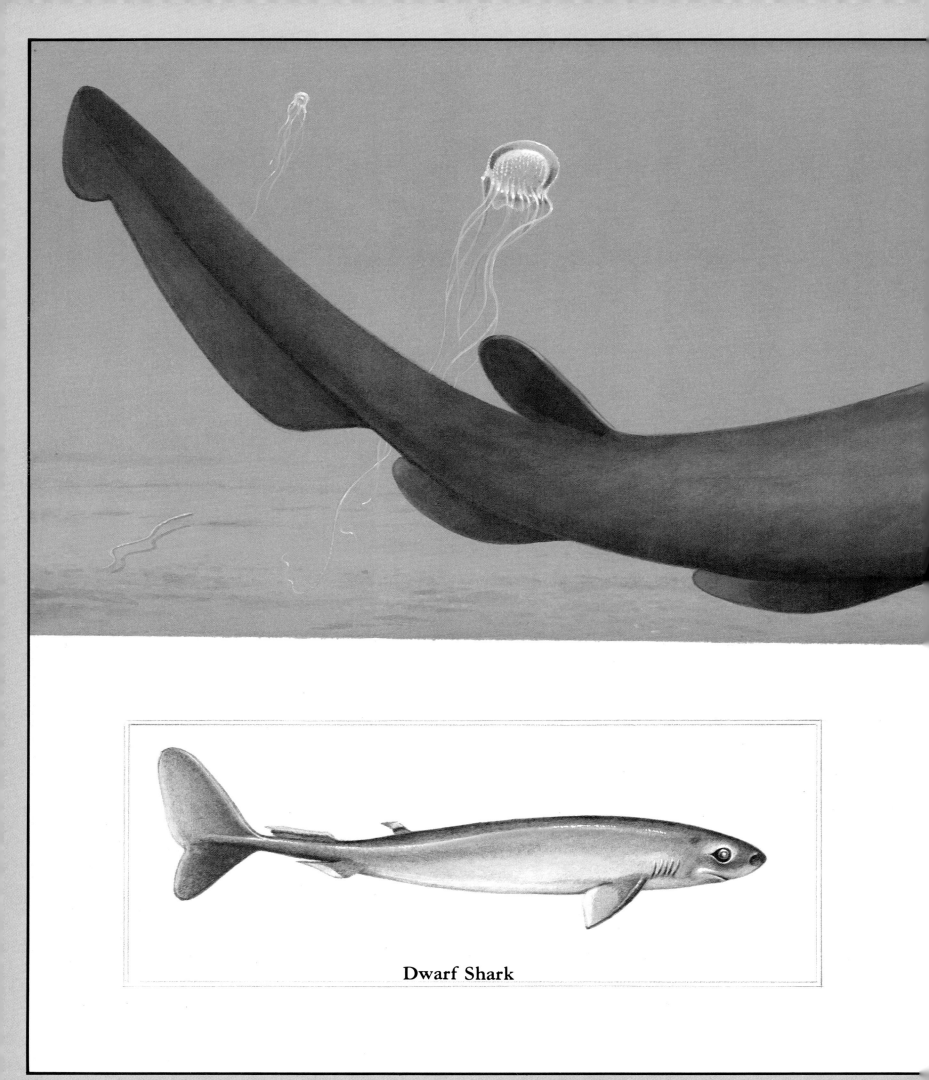

Dwarf Shark

Goblin Shark

The GOBLIN SHARK has an ugly-looking nose that sticks out past the tip of its snout. The fishermen who caught the first specimen off the coast of Japan were so shocked by its weird looks that they named it goblin shark.

Goblin sharks are very rare. The few that have been caught were found in very deep waters near Japan and South Africa. Just recently, one was caught off Suriname in South America. Scientists found out in a curious way that they also live in the Indian Ocean. A telegraph cable a mile below the surface of the Indian Ocean was damaged. When they lifted the cable out of the water, they found the sharp, pointed tooth of a goblin shark still stuck in the wire covering.

The last shark you will meet is one of the smallest of the shark family. Can you imagine a full-grown shark that is only six inches long? We're talking about the DWARF SHARK, also known as the CIGAR SHARK. In Japan, this shark has a name almost as long as its body, *tsuranagakobitozame,* which means "dwarf shark with long face." The dwarf is a rare species. It was discovered in 1908 in the waters off the Philippine Islands.

Whether they are big or little, shy or bold, round or flat, dark or brightly colored, sharks are amazing animals indeed. They are also the most feared of all wild creatures—on land or in the sea. To know about sharks is to admire and respect them.

Index

About the Author

Gilda Berger is a well-known children's book author with over twenty titles on science and other subjects to her credit. She grew up in New York City where she received her BS and MS degrees in education from the City University of New York. After several years of teaching retarded and emotionally disturbed children and developing reading material for their use, Ms. Berger decided to devote herself to writing full-time.

Both she and her author-husband, Melvin Berger, have traveled extensively along the Atlantic, Pacific, and Gulf coasts of the United States, and in the Caribbean Sea, visiting aquariums and oceanographic labs, sailing, snorkeling, and observing the fascinating life in the sea. In the course of their explorations they have caught sight of many sharks, ranging from good-sized tiger and blue sharks to schools of small dogfish.

The Bergers live in Great Neck, New York.

About the Artist

Christopher Santoro received his bachelor's degree in fine arts from the Rhode Island School of Design in 1970 and has been illustrating children's books ever since. His lavish watercolors have appeared in close to twenty books published by major houses, many of them on animals and nature-related subjects. His work has been exhibited by both the American Institute of Graphic Arts and the Society of Illustrators. One of Mr. Santoro's most recent titles appeared on *The New Yorker*'s "Best Books for Christmas 1985" list.

The artist lives in New York City with his cat, Moose, and his dog, Harry.

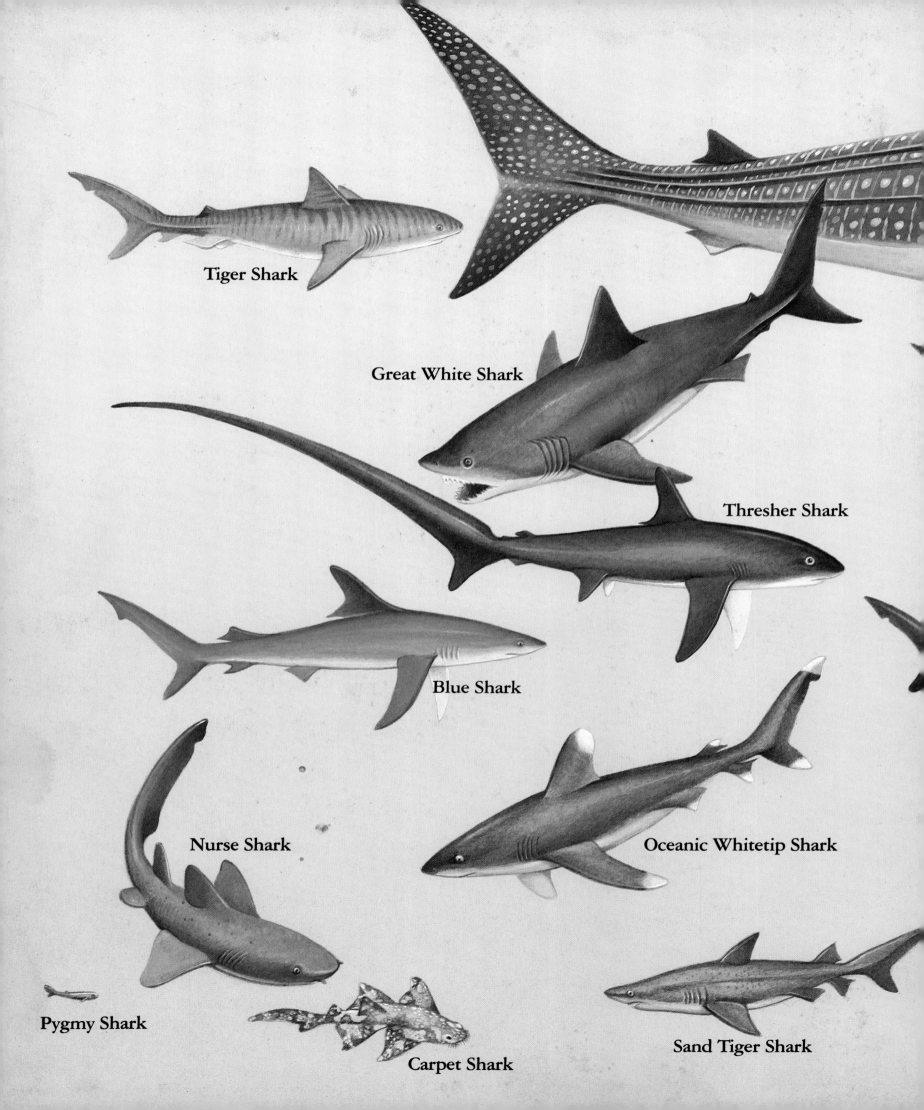

Tiger Shark

Great White Shark

Thresher Shark

Blue Shark

Nurse Shark

Oceanic Whitetip Shark

Pygmy Shark

Carpet Shark

Sand Tiger Shark